How to Write
for the
Christian Marketplace

Jo Huddleston and Vickie Phelps

How to Write for the Christian Marketplace
Copyright © 1999, 2011, 2012
by Jo Huddleston and Vickie Phelps
All rights reserved.

Cover design: Judie Moffett
Interior design: Ellen C. Maze, The Author's Mentor, ellencmaze.com

ISBN-13: 978-1475048599
Also available in eBook

PRINTED IN THE UNITED STATES OF AMERICA

Table of Contents

About the Authors

Jo Huddleston

Jo Huddleston is the author of four published nonfiction books: **Amen and Good Morning, God: A Book of Morning Prayers** and **Amen and Good Night, God: A Book of Evening Prayers** (both published by Tyndale House, 1995); **His Awesome Majesty: Praising God's Greatness** (Hendrickson Publishers, 1997), and **America: Her Hope for the Future** (CreateSpace, 2012). She coauthored a book with Vickie Phelps, **How to Write for the Christian Marketplace** (Booklocker.com, 1999).

She has placed over 200 articles, short stories, and devotionals in more than fifty different Christian and general publications, including national magazines *Guideposts*, *Decision*, and *The Upper Room*. Huddleston is a contributing author to eight anthologies and wrote an inspirational newspaper column for seven years. She speaks to women's groups, teaches at writers' conferences, and is a contributing writer for Christian Devotions Ministries (www.christiandevotions.us), an international daily devotional.

Huddleston holds a B.A. degree from Lincoln Memorial University (TN), and a M.Ed. degree from Mississippi State University.

She is a member of the American Christian Fiction Writers (ACFW) and a member of the Literary Hall of Fame at Lincoln Memorial University (TN).

Vickie Phelps

Vickie Phelps has been writing since 1988. Her published works include the following:

Vickie was part of a group of writers who worked on **Life's Simple Guide to Happiness** released by Faith Words of the Hachette Book Group in 2007. This guide serves as a devotional for the un-churched.

365 Treasured Moments for Mothers & Daughters, a perpetual calendar, Barbour Publishing, 2007.

A series of gift books was released by Barbour Publishing: **Simple Pleasures**, (2004); **Star of Wonder**, (2003); **101 Things to be Thankful for**, (2003); **May Christ be the Center of Your Christmas**, (2001); **101 Keys for Life**, (2000). **101 Keys for Life** made the Christian Booksellers Bestseller List for gift books in 2000.

An e-book, **How to Write for the Christian Marketplace** released in 1999 from Booklocker.com. Two other e-books followed soon after: **Writing 101** and **A Christmas Scrapbook**. These were coauthored with Jo Huddleston.

Phelps' writing is included in several anthologies including, **The Best of the Proverbs 31 Ministry** from The Proverbs 31 Ministry, **Seasons of a Woman's Heart** from Starburst Publishers, **The Writers' Journal Guide to the Writing Life**, from Writers' Journal Books, **A Cup of Comfort Cookbook** from Adams Media, **For Better or Worse** from Christian Publications, Inc., **God's Little Rule Book** from Starburst Publishers, and **A Treasure Box**, a publication of the Northeast Texas Writers Organization from Pennant publishing.

Over 150 articles published in publications such as *Woman's Touch*, *East Texas People*, *Lutheran Woman*

Today, Writers' Journal, Christian Education Counselor, Church of God Evangel, Christian Standard, Mature Living, Longview News Journal, Canadian Writers' Journal, Evangel, The War Cry, Lutheran Journal, The Dollar Stretcher, and *CBN.com.*

Vickie teaches at conferences and serves on the planning committee for an annual conference held at East Texas Baptist University.

Vickie is a member of the Northeast Texas Writers Organization, a charter member of the online writer's group, The Writers View and the founder of East Texas Christian Writers Group. She is also the book buyer for an independent bookstore where she has been employed for sixteen years.

Preface

We want to help other writers attain their goal of writing for the Christian marketplace. Because you're reading this book, you probably have a desire to write and be published in this field. Together, we will work toward that goal. By submitting quality writing in a professional manner, you may see your name and your stories in print in Christian periodicals. This book is to help you do that.

Introduction

How to Write for the Christian Marketplace will show you how to write for Christian publications. When we started writing in this field, we learned as we went along. Our instructions came from writing courses, attending writers' conferences, and practicing the craft.

We followed what we learned and honed our writing skills. Then we sent our manuscripts out to publishers in the Christian field. Together, we have sold our work to over 400 different periodicals.

Writing for the Christian marketplace means reaching out to others through your written words. You will be able to touch people around the world with your message. Opportunities abound to share personal experiences and encourage others in their daily life.

Now, by studying this book you can learn about many areas of the Christian writing field. Writing is a craft. Sharpen your skills and learn from our experience. Then you, too, may see your writing and your name in print in the Christian marketplace.

I

Getting Started

Getting It Down and Sending It Out

Have you ever read a book or a magazine article and said, "I could have written that"? Do you have a desire to help others by sharing your experiences? Maybe you have a knack for telling stories. If so, why not put those experiences and stories in writing? Let's get started.

Tools You Will Need:

- ✓ Computer w/printer
- ✓ Good grade of paper (20 or 24 lb. Bond is recommended.)
- ✓ #10 envelopes
- ✓ 9x12 manila envelopes
- ✓ Bible, dictionary, and thesaurus
- ✓ Market Guide

Getting Started

For some, the hardest part of writing is making the decision to get started. Interferences abound to keep you from sitting down at the keyboard and beginning to write. So set aside some time in which you will do nothing but write. It may be a good idea to write down the designated time on the calendar. In other words, make an appointment with your keyboard. You may not have large blocks of time to devote to the craft, but the important thing is using the time to write whether it be thirty minutes or an entire afternoon.

How Do I Begin?

One way to begin is by writing down your ideas for the article, poem, or story you wish to tell. Some writers make outlines, others simply write the story as if they were telling it to a friend. Still others make a list of points they wish to cover in the article and then begin to write about each point. Follow the way that works best for you. Many established writers query an editor with an idea before they ever write their article. (See Item 2 on query letters.) They sell before writing. This saves them valuable time. But if you're a beginning writer, you may want to practice the craft of writing before you begin contacting an editor.

Rewriting/Revising

Once you've written your story, put it aside for a few days. Then go back and read the manuscript you've written. You may discover points you need to cover in more detail, misspelled words, or incomplete sentences. You will need to do some rewriting and revising, making sure your manuscript is clear and focused. Will the reader understand what you're trying to say? Who is the story written for? Does it speak to the audience for which it's intended? If the answer is no to any of these questions, rewrite your story until you can answer yes. Make sure you use correct grammar, punctuation, and spelling. Editors want to see your best work.

Manuscript Format

Once you've finished writing your article or story, type your manuscript in the format shown in the sample. Remember these tips when typing your manuscript:

1. Use one-inch margins at the top, bottom and sides of your manuscript.
2. Double-space your manuscript except for the name and address information at the top. This area is single-spaced. Your word

processing programs can create this, known as a header.

3. Type your manuscript in clean, black print.

4. Don't use fancy fonts on your manuscript. Times New Roman or Courier 12 point are both acceptable.

5. Use the name and address where you receive correspondence or you want your check mailed. You may include a fax number or email address if you have either.

6. Your word processing program should give you your manuscript's word count.

7. Rights offered are the rights you are offering to sell to the editor for this particular manuscript. (See Item 3 for more information on rights.)

Sample Manuscript First Page

Name   Word Count
Address   Rights Offered
City, State, Zip
Telephone #
Email

                         Title

                      Your Name

Your story begins here.

On the second page and each consecutive page, type your last name and the title of the manuscript in the upper left corner. Type the page number in the upper right corner. Your word processing program can create this header for you. Examples:

Doe/Title   2.

Or

Doe   2.
Title

Do I Need A Cover Letter?

Some editors prefer a cover letter with your manuscript, some do not. In your cover letter, introduce yourself, list any writing credits you may have, and give a brief statement about your manuscript. If you have a degree or experience that qualifies you to write the article be sure to include that information also. Try to keep your cover letter to one page. Keep it brief and to the point.

Sending It Out

Once you've completed your manuscript, including rewriting and revising to make it as professional as possible, you're ready to submit it to a publication.

Some editors require a query letter before you submit the article to them. (See Item 2 on queries.) Others want to see a completed manuscript. You must study your market guide and the magazine guidelines to see which method the editor prefers. Writers' guidelines give additional information on what the magazine publishes, their goal or mission, payment information, and any other details specific to that particular publication. To obtain writers' guidelines, contact the magazine or go to the publication's website and request them before sending anything to that editor. It's also a good idea to study back issues of the magazine you want to submit to. In doing so, you will see if your article/story fits the magazine's profile. Be sure to follow the guidelines precisely. If the editor only wants 800 words, don't submit 1,200. If he requires a query letter, query before sending your work. By not following the guidelines as stated you will probably have your manuscript rejected and returned to you.

Simultaneous Submissions

Some publications will accept simultaneous submissions, which means you may send your work to more than one market at a time. If you decide to follow this route, check the guidelines and market guide. Be sure that each market you are submitting to accepts simultaneous submissions. On the first page of your manuscript, below "rights offered," type Simultaneous Submission. This lets the editor know you have submitted it to other places for consideration.

Multiple Submissions

Multiple submissions means the editor will look at more than one manuscript at the same time. If you want to send an editor two or more pieces of your work, be sure he accepts multiple submissions and that all work sent fits the publication's format.

What Is the SASE?

When you've chosen your market, you're ready to send a query letter or a manuscript. If you mail your submission it's important to choose the right size envelope for mailing your manuscript. If your manuscript is a short filler, poem, or a 2-3 page article, you may use a #10 business envelope to mail your work. Any more than this, you should use a 9x12 manila envelope and mail your work flat. Be sure to enclose your SASE with the manuscript. This is a self-addressed, stamped envelope for the editor's reply. If you want your manuscript returned, be sure you enclose an envelope the same size as your outer envelope. If you're only interested in a reply, a #10 envelope is sufficient. If you fail to send the SASE, most editors will simply toss your work without reading it. Editors receive hundreds of manuscripts every week. They can't afford to pay postage for responding to each one.

It's your responsibility to see that you get a reply to your query or manuscript by including the SASE. Be sure you have correct postage on that reply envelope as well as the envelope you're sending out. If you're unsure of the postage, let postal employees weigh it for you.

Many publishers only accept electronic query or manuscript submissions. Check their guidelines. You should be sure to include your contact information.

It's Gone, Now What?

Once you've submitted your manuscript or query, don't sit waiting for a reply. It may be several weeks or even months before you hear from the editor. (Guidelines and market guides usually state an approximate response time.) Now is the time to start writing your next idea. Forget about that first manuscript and get busy on another story.

What's a Query Letter, Anyway?

Some publications request that you send your completed manuscript to them for consideration to publish. Others require a query letter only. Make sure you send those editors the best query letter you can write.

What is a Query Letter?

A query letter is a sales pitch to an editor to interest him in your story. When you begin your query letter, think about TV commercials that advertise everything from cars to candy. These TV commercials are short, simple and sharply focused on the product they are selling.

Your query letter should also be narrowly focused on one idea and be to the point. Keep your letter simple, avoiding generalizations and wordiness. Your query letter should be one page of single-spaced typing.

Why Write a Query Letter?

Writing query letters will save you time and money. Why write the entire article without knowing if an editor will want your manuscript? Spending money on envelopes, postage, and trips to the post office could be a waste at this point.

Sending a complete manuscript to an editor who requires a query letter usually results in a quick rejection of an unread manuscript. An editor would think twice about working with a writer who can't follow simple rules of submission requirements.

Writing a query can also avoid rejection because of editorial commitments or preferences. The editor may have just assigned an article on your topic. Or, she may like your article idea but want you to write it with a different slant. Because you haven't written the manuscript, you can easily do this. If you had completed the article you would need to start all over in order to work with this editor. Why waste all that time?

Be ready to write your article – then write your query letter. Have everything you need to write the article – all research should be complete.

What's in a Query Letter?

Begin your query letter with an opening that coaxes the editor to read farther. You may find later that you will use this opening as the beginning of your article. In your opening, don't try to be cute or use gimmicks; this is a business letter. Be professional; put your best foot forward. Simply and quickly come to the point and state your article idea. You may offer a working title for the article, but an editor often changes titles.

Next, explain and summarize the article you propose to write. If you have statistics supporting your topic, you can include an important one here. You can list the areas you plan to cover in the article. Mention the word length of your article, being sure to stay within the word limits of the publication you are contacting. Tell the editor when you could have the article finished.

Continue your query with a paragraph about your qualifications to write this article. If you're writing about accidents around a swimming pool and you are a lifeguard, this will show your authority to do this article. If you have publishing credits, list a few of the major ones. If you haven't been published yet, don't mention it.

In the letter's last paragraph, indicate your enthusiasm for your article idea and for this editor to consider publishing it in his magazine. Thank the editor for his or her time. You can end your letter by writing that you look forward to hearing from him or her – or end with a question "...would you be interested in this article?" (See sample query letter)

Make it Mistake-free

If you can organize and write an interest-grabbing query letter, it will help the editor decide whether you are capable of writing the article. Your query letter needs to be free of mistakes. This letter is the editor's only way to evaluate you as a writer.

You want to make a good first impression of you and your writing. If your letter has typographical errors and grammatical goofs, why would he allow you to write for his professional magazine?

Submitting Your Work

Send your query to a specific editor by name. You can find this information on their website or in their guidelines.

When your query results in an acceptance of your idea, complete your assigned article and send it to the editor by the agreed deadline. In your cover letter be sure to write that you are sending the article at his request. If you're not submitting electronically, on the outside of the 9x12 envelope write "Requested Material." This will keep your article from falling into the stacks of unsolicited manuscripts waiting to be read.

Sometimes an editor will phone to give you the go-ahead to write the article. In this case, follow up your conversation with a letter or email confirming your understanding of the terms of the assignment. Many magazines do not issue contracts and this confirmation letter from you will substitute for a contract.

SAMPLE QUERY LETTER

JO PHELPS
123 Main Street, Anywhere, Any State 55555
Phone 555-555-5555, joph@xweb.com

Date

Mr. Anxious Johnson, Editor
General Travel Magazine
234 Any Street
Somewhere, NY 55555

Dear Mr. Johnson:

Would you be interested in a 1200-word article for *General Travel* about Gulf Shores, Alabama and the thirty-two miles of Alabama's Gulf Coast? The area is conducive to summer vacations, spring or fall weekends, or a winter's stay to enjoy subtropical climate. The article would cover available lodging, ranging from campgrounds to high-rise condominiums, and would include points of interest and entertainment.

I've published over thirty articles in more than twenty magazines. My travel articles have appeared in such magazines as *The Saturday Evening Post* and *Travel and Leisure*. I will include photographs to accompany the article, which I could have to you by the end of August.

This article would be appropriate for your readers since they are retirees with time and money to travel. Please let me know if you're interested in my writing this article.

Sincerely,

Jo Phelps

I'm Selling What Rights?

When you write a magazine article, short story, or poem, you own the rights to that work. When you get ready to sell that work to a publication, you agree to sell certain rights to them. Always be aware of what rights you are selling to any publisher that wants to use your work. It may mean not being able to use that piece again in printed form.

Types of Rights

❖ **First Rights:** The writer offers the publication the right to publish a manuscript for the first time in print. Writer retains all other rights to the manuscript.

❖ **First North American Rights:** Some publishers distribute in both Canada and the United States. They buy these rights to cover publishing in both countries.

❖ **One-Time Rights:** The writer offers the publisher the right to publish the work one time. This can be either first or second rights.

❖ **Reprint Rights (Second Rights):** Writer offers the publisher the right to reprint a work that has been published elsewhere.

❖ **All Rights:** The publisher is buying all rights to the work. The writer gives up all rights to the work in its present form.

❖ **Simultaneous Rights:** These are sold to publications that do not have overlapping circulations. Some Christian markets will buy these because their publication is strictly for their denomination and will not be affected by another publication's circulation.

❖ **Electronic Rights:** Electronic rights is the right to publish your work in an electronic format. As a part of the sale, a lot of markets also purchase electronic rights at the time they purchase print rights. They may or may not give you extra payment for electronic rights, but it may be included in the purchase as part of the print rights.

Writers should always be aware of what rights they're selling to their work. Some publications will send you a contract or agreement to sign and return giving them permission to print your work. Whenever possible, you should retain the reprint rights to your work. This allows you to sell the work to other publications and earn extra money or use the work in some other way. The contract/agreement should state the rights you are selling. If you don't receive a contract/agreement, check the market guide to see what rights the publisher buys or ask the editor. Signing and cashing a check from a publisher signifies your acceptance of their policies. So know what rights you're selling before you cash that check.

Keeping Records

Why Keep Writing Records?

Even if your writing "office" is at the kitchen table, you need organization in that cardboard box you move from your closet to the table. To be useful, your writing records and material should be organized and kept in an orderly manner. Lost records will be of no use to you. If you don't organize your writing material, you'll probably experience mild panic at times in your writing career.

What Records to Keep

❖ **Submissions.** If serious about writing for publication, all writers need to keep track of their submissions. Some do this by using 3x5 cards in a card file box; others keep submission data in a notebook; and still others keep them in file folders or a computer program such as Excel. Whichever way you choose, certain submission items are essential in your records.

The form for keeping this information doesn't need to be elaborate. I'm still using the same "Submission Log" form I worked up for myself years ago. Set up a form that will serve your needs. Make a note of these items on your form: the date you submitted your article; article's title; name of the magazine submitted to; date you should have a response from them (get this from their guidelines or a market guide – see Writing Helps in Chapter III); date you receive their response; and whether the article was accepted or rejected.

❖ **Articles.** Keep a copy of each article you write and place each into a separate file folder. Along with the article, include a second form that holds information on this article only. At the top of this form, put the name of this article and the word count for easy future reference. You'll need to keep the date of each time you send out this article, the publication where you send it, date of any response, acceptance or rejection, and the date and payment you receive for accepted manuscripts.

Keeping accurate submission information in these ways will let you track your articles. At a glance, you can see what's still out and when you should hear from the publication.

❖ **Magazine copies and guidelines.** You can now go online to read some magazines and obtain guidelines. For those publications that are not online you may have to write and request sample copies and their writers' guidelines. When you receive sample copies and guidelines by mail you need to store them orderly. Again, using a cardboard box or file cabinet, set aside room to file alphabetically. Place one copy of each magazine, along with its guidelines, in individual folders. It will be easy for you to refer to when article ideas come to you. Keep your guidelines up-to-date. Old guidelines aren't of much benefit. Date them when you get them.

Be careful not to keep every magazine and guideline. Some of them will not be in your area of interest and you can better use the valuable space they would take up if you kept them.

* ❖ **Correspondence.** Keep copies of all letters of correspondence, emails, and phone call notes about an article *with* that article. However, you may have other miscellaneous correspondence. You can set up a single file folder and put all these letters together alphabetically. As your writing career grows, you will probably need to expand this. You could then file your correspondence by topics – for example, correspondence with editors, with writing friends, etc. Or, you could simply set up a file for each letter of the alphabet and file your letters and notes there alphabetically by last names of correspondents.

* ❖ **Ideas.** When you get an idea for a writing project, jot it down right then, even if on the back of your hand! Keep a note pad and pencil by your bedside to write down those fabulous ideas that will come to you on the brink of sleep. You may think you'll remember the idea the next morning. More than

likely, though, you won't. If you don't write it down, the idea may well be gone forever. Another idea is to record your thoughts on a recorder or on your cell phone if it has the capability.

Ideas may be written on the backs of envelopes, fast-food sacks, and grocery receipts. Drop them all into an "Ideas" file folder and find a place for the folder in your filing system.

When you have more thoughts about one of these ideas, make more notes, put them together with your original note, and set up a file folder for this idea alone. Now you have a place to drop a pertinent quotation or statistic you may run across. On those days you feel drained of all creativity, go to these folders and pull out any idea to jump-start your writing.

Keeping records is simple once you devote time to setting up an orderly system. You'll be glad you did when that editor phones to talk about the article you sent her and you can locate it and have it in front of you as you talk.

Writing is a business. Keep your records in a businesslike and professional manner.

II

Writing Opportunities

Touching Your Readers Through Devotionals

Successful writers strive to touch their readers and prompt them to action or reaction. An effective way to do this is through writing devotionals. When a particular subject has influenced you, you have a passion you can share through a devotional.

However, the devotional is not your avenue to preach to your reader or to be judgmental. If this is your agenda when you write a devotional, you will likely lose the reader's attention soon after she begins reading your article.

Writing devotionals will give you opportunities to offer your reader hope, not a sermon. Avoid using words like *must*, *should*, and *ought*. Also avoid lofty and theological vocabulary. The devotional is not a formal paper. Write clear and precise prose from an ordinary person's viewpoint.

Devotionals, sometimes called meditations, fall into the category of a quick read. Don't be misled, however, into thinking that short on length endorses the absence of quality writing. Devotionals should meet the same requirements of good writing as any other manuscript worthy of publication.

Format

The format of your devotional may vary from magazine to magazine. Word length may also vary but not to a great extent. Meditations known as *daily* devotionals usually contain about 250 words and have similar format. Meditations other than daily devotionals can range upwards to 600 words.

Most devotionals begin with a Bible verse, followed by the story narration and application and usually end with a one- or two-line prayer that summarizes the entire devotional. Before you start writing your devotional know your target publication's specific format and word length requirements as stated in their guidelines.

Passion and Emotion

Devotionals that impact your reader are ones you write from your heart, not your head. Yes, your ideas begin in your head but if you don't have passion for that idea in your heart, you won't touch your reader as well as you can when the passion is present. Devotional writing must be sincere and honest; don't try to fake the passion. You can't. Readers can spot a phony.

When you begin your devotional, you will have your idea first but you already will have experienced a compelling emotion about this idea. And the idea, combined with your compelling emotion about it, forms a powerful devotional.

Insight

In your devotional, write about common things that are known to most people. Don't use an example unfamiliar to a general audience.

Through a devotional, you can give your reader meaningful insight into commonplace situations. Be attentive to what's happening around you and discover how stories in the Bible pertain to your activities.

Focus

The focus of a devotional is narrow. With its length restrictions, the devotional can't take your reader through the entire Bible, from Genesis to Revelation. You don't have time to tell what Adam, Moses, David, and the twelve disciples thought about your topic. To focus in your devotional is like looking through a telescope. You can't see an entire galaxy, but look at one star at a time. Each devotional should focus on only one point.

The Take-Away

A well-written devotional can offer your reader encouragement in his circumstances. Give him a "take-away," something beneficial in your story that he can use in his everyday living. Through your devotionals, you can touch your reader on an emotional level, an experience he won't soon forget.

Everyday incidents can remind us of how God works in lives. Perhaps you have discovered a special meaning from a Bible verse you've studied. Maybe God has become real to you while working through a difficult situation.

You can share your feelings and discoveries with your readers so they may apply what you've experienced to their lives. An impressive devotional has a take-away value for your readers that is meaningful not only immediately, but for days and weeks to come.

Audience

The audience for devotionals is widespread when published in some daily devotionals. A popular daily devotional guide, *The Upper Room*, is read or listened to by eight to ten million people in forty different languages.

Marketing Your Devotional

When you look in market guides you will find an extensive listing of religious magazines. Some of them state a need for "inspirational" articles, which sometimes can be interpreted to mean devotional-type articles. Read the information given for each magazine and request writers' guidelines from those periodicals that interest you. Be sure to enclose your SASE for a reply if you request by mail.

Many selections for daily devotionals are written on assignment only. When you choose a daily devotional you want to write for, send a brief letter stating your interest in writing for them. Ask how you can gain an assignment. Some use only writers from their denomination, and aren't easily deceived if you try to write like you are one of them when you aren't.

Many daily devotionals use first-time writers. They publish 365 meditations each year, making this market more open to writers than some.

Rights Offered

Appearing in several publications lessens the impact of the short but widely distributed daily devotional. For that reason, when you write on assignment for daily devotional publications, expect them to ask for all rights to your manuscript. When deciding whether you want to relinquish your rights, weigh the value to you of the vast audience you will touch and the reach of your story to affect people's lives.

Getting Paid

Although great monetary wealth is unusual when selling your devotionals, the opportunities for Christian ministry are great. Because of circulation into the hundreds of thousands, a writer of devotionals can reach far more readers and touch many more lives than a first printing of a book that is usually 5,000-20,000 copies. Your story in the Billy Graham Association's *Decision* magazine will reach almost 2 million people and *The Lookout* magazine's circulation exceeds 100,000.

Why write devotionals? Through a good devotional, you can give your readers hope and encouragement to help them in their daily lives. After reading your devotional, readers can identify with your main idea and perhaps say, "I never knew anyone else felt like this."

Write your devotional well, and it will touch your reader and help him to deal with life's situations.

Writing Fillers for Print and Profit

Writing fillers is a good way to break into print for the first time or to open doors at a new market. At one time, magazines only used fillers to fill up blank space at the end of a page. Now almost all periodicals use fillers in some form and they're used as regular features in some magazines.

What are Fillers?

Poems, recipes, craft ideas, quotes, cartoons, household hints, puzzles, and jokes are all forms of fillers. Short prose of 50-500 words is also used as filler in some magazines. Length depends on the magazine so study their guidelines.

Ideas for Fillers

Where do you get your ideas for fillers? Do you have a hobby? Are you a gourmet cook? For thirteen years, I worked in a bakery as a cake decorator. I used my experience to write a recipe for decorating a Christmas wreath cake. *Woman's Touch*, a Christian woman's magazine, published it in a December issue. Can you describe a humorous incident at work or write a short description for a how-to page? Can you give someone tips on how to improve their prayer life or how to get more out of their Bible study? All of these ideas can be turned into short prose items for magazine fillers.

Slice-of-life episodes are a good source for fillers. One afternoon in the middle of August, I locked myself out of the house. Since we live in the country, there was nothing to do but wait outside in the heat until my husband got home from work. Using that experience, I wrote a short devotional and sold it to *Christian Herald*.

Keep an idea file. A spiral notebook or a recipe card file will work well. When an idea strikes, write it down. Jot down bumper stickers and funny incidents that happen with the kids.

Reading can inspire ideas for fillers, too. Pick up some sample issues of your favorite magazines or examine the ones you receive at church, by subscription, or check online. What kinds of items do they publish? Do they have a regular short feature or a poetry page?

Seasonal ideas make great fillers. Use the four seasons or the holidays to write recipes, poems, puzzles, or short prose. One way to come up with ideas for holiday fillers is word association. Make a list of words associated with the holiday. Write the holiday or season at the top of the page, then begin listing every word you associate with that time. For example: Christmas: Christ, snow, trees, nativity, carols, sleigh bells, frankincense, candles, and on and on. Certain words may trigger special memories for you to write about.

Remember these tips when you write holiday fillers:

1. Seasonal material must be submitted well in advance of the holiday you choose to write about. Editors work months in advance of their publication date. Check writers' guidelines for lead time so your article won't arrive too late to be considered for the proper season.

2. Study your markets carefully to see which ones buy seasonal material.

3. Keep a calendar close to your computer and keep it turned six to eight months ahead. Write about the holidays or seasons listed for the month showing on your advanced calendar.

Tips for Writing Fillers

Just because it's a filler doesn't mean you can submit mediocre work to an editor. Editors appreciate well-written material of any kind. And this may be your best chance to break into their magazines, so make a good impression.

1. Type your filler and double-space it.
2. Check spelling, grammar, and punctuation.
3. Type one filler per page unless the publication's guidelines give you permission to do otherwise.
4. Be sure your subject matter fits the publication.
5. Stay within the specified word limit.
6. Include an appropriate-sized SASE with your filler if a hard copy is required.

Writing for the Local Church

Do you enjoy writing poetry or keeping a journal? Are you interested in seeing some of your work in print? Maybe you're one of those people who write and stash it in a drawer or on the closet shelf because you think no one is interested in what you have to say.

If you're interested in writing and seeing your words in print, why not write for your church? You may not receive monetary payment but there are other rewards.

This is good writing experience if you're trying to break into the writing field and a good way to receive feedback from people who read your articles. A comment from a former pastor about an article I wrote encouraged me to start writing and submitting to other publications.

Getting Started

The first step to writing for your church is to contact the editor of your church newsletter or bulletin. If you have samples of your writing, take them along when you meet with the editor.

Most of the articles used in church newsletters or bulletins are fillers. They are usually short articles about one of the members, church events, inspirational pieces, or poems. The editor may assign you an article or allow you to write one of your own choosing. Be sure to ask about word limits and special themes for future issues.

What to Write

❖ **Personality Profiles**: If you attend a large church, do a profile piece on a different staff member each week to better acquaint the congregation with the leaders of the church.

❖ **New Member Profiles:** When a new family or individual joins your church, arrange an interview with them and write a short profile to acquaint the other church members with newcomers.

❖ **Church Events:** What's going on in the church? Write an article on mission projects being undertaken by the church, upcoming events, special speakers, or class reports from each class or department in the church.

❖ **Devotionals:** Ask the editor about writing a devotional each week, focusing on a different age group each time.

❖ **Poems:** These can be religious or inspirational in content. Ask the editor about poems with other themes.

❖ **Book Reviews:** This column could be used to inform church members of new books in the church library or those available at the local bookstore. Of course, this would mean reading the book yourself before writing.

❖ **Puzzles, Quizzes, and Cartoons:** Ask the editor about including these items in the bulletin. They should have a religious theme or be church related.

These are only a few of the topics you could use. The editor may have others or you may think of a subject you would like to write about.

Other Opportunities

Don't overlook other opportunities to write for your church. Teachers, youth workers, and staff members need written material. They may need handouts, skits, devotionals, lesson summaries, Bible stories, or poems to accompany their class work. Some of the children's teachers might like to have short stories to share with their class.

Most churches belong to a denominational organization. You might act as your church reporter and write a report for the state or regional publication each month. Check with your pastor about this first. The list is endless and there is opportunity to serve your church if you want to take advantage of the ministry of writing for others.

Starting a Church Newsletter

If your church doesn't have a newsletter or church bulletin, you might consider starting one yourself. The first step is to talk with your pastor. If he or she is open to the idea, here are some questions you need to ask.

❖ Does the church have some method of printing the newsletter?

❖ How much money will you be allowed to spend?

❖ How often will the newsletter be published? Weekly, monthly?

❖ How long will the publication be? (Determined in part, by the budget.)

❖ What type of material will be included in the newsletter?

Once you have your pastor's approval, you can begin work. The length of your publication will determine how much material you need. If there are other writers in the church, enlist their help in writing material.

One Last Note

Be aware of copyrighted material. You need permission to use these works. If you don't have enough original material, there are publications written to aid you in putting together an article.

Writing the How-To Article

If you're reading this book, then you're interested in learning how to write for the Christian market. Lots of other people are interested in learning how to do new things or how to improve their lifestyle. For that reason, editors are looking for good how-to articles.

What Can I Write About?

The best way to get started writing how-to articles is to write about what you already know. If you've been successful at working with children, you can probably give tips on how to keep a child's attention during story time. If you're trained in a special trade, you have experience that others may want to know and read about. How do you spend your leisure time? Have you raised children? These questions can result in ideas for how-to articles, but remember that Christian markets are looking for the how-to that will inspire and teach from a Christian viewpoint.

Once you've exhausted ideas from your own experiences or knowledge, don't stop writing. By doing research, you can become knowledgeable on lots of subjects and write about them, too. Don't limit your research to reading. Interview people in the field you want to write about – they can give you tips you might never pick up by reading.

Getting Started

Give your article a catchy title. You can always call it "How To," but a unique title will catch an editor's eye and later, the reader's attention. "Ten Minutes a Day Keeps the Blues Away," is more interesting than "How to Pray Ten Minutes a Day."

Open your article with an introduction on the subject you're writing about. This doesn't need to be a long paragraph – just a few short sentences to get your reader started in the right direction. Next, start listing your steps to do the project you're writing about, beginning with step number one and progressing to the final step. Be sure to give clear directions.

Write tight. In other words, tell your reader only what he needs to know to accomplish the task. Once you've finished giving the reader the information needed, finish with a short paragraph to close the article or simply end the article with the last step. How much you write will depend on the publication's word limit.

Who Reads How-To Articles?

Children, teens, men, and women all read how-to articles. Lots of people enjoy craft articles. A women's magazine might be interested in a needlework article or how to teach your child to pray. A children's publication would be interested in an article on how to teach your dog a trick. Just be sure your article is on a subject that will interest that age group.

Marketing

When you get ready to market your how-to article, study guidelines and your market guide to see which publications buy how-to material. Remember to gear your article to the publication's readership. A publication that deals specifically with prayer won't be interested in how to decorate your home for Christmas, but a Christian women's magazine might be looking for that very subject to print in their December issue. Know your publication before submitting to it.

Only You Can Write a Personal Experience Article

In the Christian marketplace, a personal experience article gives readers biblical insight that relates to them and their circumstance. They provide needed encouragement to get through difficult situations.

Making Them Suitable

Appropriate personal experience articles in the Christian marketplace will result in strong reader identification. Your readers must see that you have been in a situation similar to theirs and you will tell them how you survived the emotional or physical problem. They look for understanding of their circumstance even if they must receive it from written words.

In your personal experience article, you're not trying to preach your reader out of their troubles. Write in a warm, conversational style directed at readers who are searching for help.

Share the lessons you have learned. These may have come from your family and extended family life, your job, and friends. From these areas you may have gleaned personal experiences to offer in your article that could be just the thing someone wants to hear.

Ideas

Personal experiences from which you gain biblical insight can come to you at any time. Be quick to record these insights when they happen; seize them immediately – for, like other literary ideas, they may vanish with time. Keep some 3x5 cards or note pads with you at all times for this purpose.

The idea for one personal experience article I wrote developed when my small child squirmed in the back seat on car trips. Before we'd leave our city limits she would ask, "How many more towns before we get there?"

I thought about how impatient we probably appear to God as we travel through life, wondering what lies ahead. Quoting Psalm 46:1 from the Bible, I applied the verse to times when we may be uncertain what's down the road in our life journey. "How Many More Towns" became a 200-word article that was published in a market for beginning writers.

Another 200-word article was about how nervous a family dog became during a thunderstorm. I told about how he paced back and forth outside a patio door, fearful about the approaching storm. This was just a story about an ordinary dog in an ordinary situation. I related it to humankind worrying instead of releasing all anxiety to God (1 Peter 5:7) and it became a personal experience article with a worthy lesson for readers.

Using Anecdotes of Faith

When you write your personal experience illustration and connect it to a Bible verse, some magazines like for you to expand your article by also tying the illustration to a specific anecdote in your life of faith.

In a 300-word article submitted to *Decision* magazine, I wrote about my granddaughter's dilemma while standing at the top of her new slide. She was unable to slide down because the metal was too hot, but she lacked necessary coordination to climb back down the steps. Her escape route was a flying leap into my arms, never doubting that I would catch her.

Although I linked my granddaughter's faith that I would catch her to biblical faith in God (Isaiah 26:4), *Decision* rejected the manuscript. They did, however, invite me to submit a rewrite if I could tie my granddaughter's problem and its resolution to something specific in my own life of faith.

In the rewrite, my original article increased to 600 words. I added how my behavior had resembled that of my granddaughter on an earlier occasion when her mother had been gravely ill. I wrote how I also had trusted God to catch me in my seemingly hopeless situation. *Decision* published "Catch Me!" as a vignette, required in their guidelines to have 400-1,000 words.

Make Them Relevant

Make your personal experience articles relevant. You might write about something that happened twenty years ago, but remember to make it relate to your reader's life today. If you don't, the reader – and the editor – can say, "So what?"

Instead, the desired reaction is, "I'm glad I read that; at last, someone understands." The well-written personal experience article gives your readers emotional support to help them handle their situations.

You have your own unique experiences to tell – no one can write about them but you. You've already worked through some things that others are trying to get through. Listen to your own heart's message and connect with your reader's emotions.

Writing Christian Fiction

Does the Christian writing field have a place for fiction? Can fiction be in harmony with biblical truth? Some liken fiction to untruths and reason that fact and fiction cannot and should not blend in the Christian marketplace.

Jesus did some of his most powerful teaching by using stories. The Bible calls them parables. Through these stories, Jesus brought home eternal lessons of Christian living relative even today. Written stories can be a vital tool in a writer's Christian witness.

Successful fiction in the Christian field and the general market share certain essential elements of good fiction. However, fiction written for the Christian field will differ in a few areas.

Common Elements of Any Fiction

Believable and appealing characters, an interesting situation, conflict, and suspense are ingredients of successful fiction. Good characterization is better revealed through dialogue, while some characterization through description can be used. Something important must happen in your story and your main character must change by the end.

When writing fiction, know from the beginning the difference between *showing* and *telling*. Telling is spending a page or two telling with narration what's happening. Showing is using dialogue and action to reveal the characters and their problems. Showing is the best way to keep the reader involved.

Essential Elements of Christian Fiction

The Christian field has a place for short fiction in many magazines. But don't mistake "short" and "for the Christian field" to mean that quality is not required. Fiction for the Christian field requires all the elements of good fiction as that written for the general market.

Insight

In addition to all the qualities of good general fiction, your fiction in this field will also include biblical insight. Weave Christian virtues into the plot of the story. As with much of Christian writing, your story is not a forum for your sermons. Let Christian principles evolve with the resolution of the main character's problems.

Characters

Your characters must have some kind of evangelical faith; however, don't let spirituality come easy for your main character. Don't make any of your characters all good or all bad. You want your reader to be able to relate with your characters, so give the good guys at least one bad trait and the bad guys at least one good one. Even Christian characters struggle with their humanity if they are believable.

Conflict

Conflict is necessary to propel any fiction, so have your main character face an obstacle or challenge within the realm of a Christian worldview of thinking. Make sure life is not easy for your main character; this gives him opportunity to grow and change by the end of the story.

Theme

Write about universal subjects, something that touches the heart of people: love, moral challenges, family relationships. Make your theme applicable to where you reader is today.

Perspective

The perspective of your Christian fiction is evangelical. Show Scripture as a foundation for our lives, that God responds to prayer, and His power is at work.

Taboos

Inherent limitations are present in fiction published in the Christian marketplace. Editors will not tolerate explicit sexual scenes, violence, cursing, and humanism.

Moral Resolution

Your story must have a moral resolution where principles of right and good triumph. Your main character must resolve his conflict and the story must have a believable resolution. Don't rely on coincidence to solve all the problems. Especially don't rely on divine miracle or intervention at just the right moment to bring about a happy ending to your story.

Forms of Fiction

Accepted forms of fiction for periodicals are the short-short story and the short story. These forms are defined by their length: a short-short story is usually 1,000-2,000 words, which is fewer than two to three printed pages, and the length of a short story is 3,500-5,000 words.

As their names imply, the short-short and short stories have limitations in length. They will have the same basic elements already discussed. The writer's challenge is packaging all these elements in a few pages. The scope of your story is limited to a short time span and centers on one important event. Short fiction usually has one plot line. You don't have words to waste on long conversations or descriptions. With limited time span and location, you can't move your characters around too much.

How Do I Begin?

Read the kind of fiction you want to write. Read the piece the first time to enjoy it. Then read the same story a second time to figure out why you liked it – what made it work. Look for patterns, those things that get repeated in each story you read. If you find out that most of the published stories in your chosen market have a lot of the same elements, you've discovered a "formula" for writing that kind of fiction.

To come up with good ideas for your stories, watch people in check-out lines; coming in and out of dressing rooms at the mall; sitting in their cars at traffic lights – everywhere. Our real life experiences give us the best research possible on which to base our fiction.

Play the "what if?" game, but don't stop with "what if." What if, in reality, you are eating in a fast food restaurant. An unkempt, elderly man enters and approaches the counter. The man apparently asks the employee if he might have something to eat. She refuses him when he indicates he has no money. The man shuffles quietly toward the door to leave.

Ask "what next?" Maybe a member of the family in your story at the restaurant will call to mind Jesus' words, "For I was hungry and you gave me nothing to eat . . . whatever you did not do for the least of these you did not do for me" (Matthew 25:31-46). Ask "what then?" The family wonders why they didn't offer to pay for the old man's meal. You have now provided conflict for this family – do they ignore the dirty man as other customers are doing? In your story, you can give a morally satisfying resolution to the family's dilemma, one that also shows a biblical perspective.

Keeping Your Reader's Interest

Ever wonder why so many people watch soap operas? They watch them day after day because they want to know what happens next. Write to make your reader want to know what happens next.

Keep your main character in conflict or trouble until the end. Build tension and suspense, tie up all the loose plot threads and end your story as soon as the conflict is settled. Hopefully your reader has been pulling for your main character and wants him to win. Therefore, a happy ending is usually more satisfying to the reader.

Getting Your Story on Paper

When you write your first draft just get your story down. Write from your feelings and emotions; don't stop to worry about grammar, spelling, etc.

First efforts can be improved. On the writing of your second draft, you can be analytical but not emotional. This time, be critical: Check the mechanics, make necessary changes, cut down wordage, tighten where possible, and weigh one word against another.

Now, set your story aside for a while so when you read it again it will appear fresher to you. Then, read your finished story aloud, especially the dialogue. This will help you to see places that don't move along smoothly. See if your dialogue sounds like real conversation. Does your story flow from scene to scene and from beginning to end? When you read your story aloud, it's more nearly what your reader will read when he sees your story for the first time.

When your story is the very best you can write, submit it for publication. See market guides for publishers who accept the kind of fiction you have written.

Let Take-Home Papers Take Your Writing Home

What Is a Take-home Paper?

A take-home paper in the Christian marketplace is a weekly publication that usually runs from four to sixteen pages. Publishers aim these inspirational papers to adults, children, teens, and young adults. As the name indicates, these papers are made available to church congregations to be taken home for reading.

What Do They Publish?

A take-home paper is a good market for fillers, personal experience articles, short devotionals, and fiction. Issued weekly, they provide many opportunities to submit your work. Some of these take-home papers use 100-200 pieces of fiction and up to fifty fillers each year.

How Do I Submit to Them?

Many are denominational in content, but do accept submissions from those outside their denomination.

Take-home papers published by various denominations seldom have overlapping distribution. Therefore, after your work has been published the first time, you may submit it to more than one of these non-competing markets at the same time. When simultaneously submitting to them, you would offer them reprint rights. In your cover letter, mention that you are offering the magazine "first reprint rights in their denomination." This will let them know you are submitting elsewhere but not to a publication that distributes to their same audience.

The take-home paper is a suitable market for any writer and an excellent market for beginning writers. Many writers get their first work published in this market.

Writing for Inspirational Magazines

Editors of inspirational magazines are looking for quality articles to inspire, inform, and encourage their readers in their Christian experience. If you want to do these same things for people, then you can write for inspirational magazines.

Types of Magazines

Inspirational: These magazines seek to inspire their readers with stories of faith in God and seeing God at work in people's lives. Markets in this area are generally Christian in nature and content, but usually aren't connected with a denominational organization. Ministries or other Christian groups may publish them. Examples: *Guideposts,* which calls itself, "A practical guide to successful living," *Decision Magazine* published by the Billy Graham organization, and *The War Cry* published by the Salvation Army.

Denominational: These magazines are published by religious denominations. The magazines contain informational articles and news of the denomination. They are doctrinal in their content. As a writer, you must not only study the guidelines for these magazines, but you need to know something about their beliefs. Examples of this group are: *Pentecostal Evangel,* published by the Assemblies of God, *Christian Standard* published by the Christian Church/Church of Christ, and *The Lutheran* published by the Lutheran denomination. Not all magazines in this category contain doctrinal articles. Some are published to provide their membership with good Christian reading material, but they will not publish articles contrary to their doctrine.

Breaking In

The best way to break into this market area is by writing for your own denomination. You're already familiar with the doctrine and know what is acceptable. You probably receive copies of the magazine at church or by subscription. Study them carefully to see the types of articles they print. Write and request a copy of their writers' guidelines or check their website. Once you know what the editor is looking for, you can submit your work to him, being sure it follows the guidelines and doctrinal standards.

Not all of the articles in the denominational magazines are doctrinal. After you have published in your own organization's publication, you may be able to submit this same article to another denomination as a reprint. Be sure there are no doctrinal statements in the article and let the editor know where you published it first.

The inspirational magazines print stories relevant to all beliefs, regardless of doctrine. Their mission is to encourage and inspire. You may be able to use some of the same material in this field as in the denominational area.

Types of Articles

What can you submit to these magazines? You'll find they print personal experience stories, devotionals, fillers, how-to articles, puzzles, poetry, and some fiction. Study each publication's guidelines to see what they buy. Read the magazines carefully. You'll soon learn which ones will accept fiction and which ones only want personal experience stories and devotionals.

Markets

Under the topics of inspirational and denominational magazines, you'll find many smaller topics. There are magazines for men, women, pastors, children, Christian education leaders, and teens. For example, the Southern Baptist denomination publishes *Journey*, a devotional magazine for women, *Living With Teenagers*, for parents of teens, and *Mature Living* for seniors. Guideposts also publishes *Sweet 16* and *Guideposts for Kids*.

So, gather your sample issues along with each publication's guidelines and get busy writing for the inspirational magazine market.

Other Writing Opportunities

We would also like to briefly mention some other writing opportunities. Don't hesitate to explore the areas listed below. They are also looking for freelancers to fill their pages.

Essays

When you think of an essay, you may remember the story you wrote the first week of elementary school each year. The teacher had you to write, "What I Did This Summer," or "My Family Vacation." As a rule, essays take one incident or event and explore that subject. Remember to keep your essay focused on the incident you want to share. Don't go rambling off on a side street. In an essay, the writer attempts to draw readers in by making them feel or sense the same feelings the writer experienced. In essence, the writer shares a small personal slice of life.

Opinion Pieces (Op/Ed)

An opinion piece is exactly what it says – your opinion. All of us feel strongly about the issues of life. We all want the opportunity to express those opinions at one time or another. Newspapers and some magazines buy opinion pieces or editorials. This is the place to share your feelings on the issue that is closest to you. You may want to let citizens in your community know how you feel about the drug problem in your city, state, or the nation. If you write a well-crafted piece, expressing your views, you may find a market right in your own hometown. This is not the place to vent, rant, and rave, declaring that everyone else is wrong. It is an opportunity to make your voice heard.

Greeting Cards

So, you don't have a desire to write the next "great American novel." Instead, you enjoy writing short notes to people. Maybe you're one of those who always adds personal verses to a greeting card. If so, then writing for the greeting card market may be your niche. It's essential that you know how to touch people and tap into their emotions. If you can do that and express those feelings on paper, you're off to a good start. Greeting card publishers have guidelines that must be followed, so be sure to check for these before you start submitting your ideas.

Writing for Children

Writing for children requires the same quality writing as the adult market. The children's market is very competitive, but there are opportunities for you. Some people make the mistake of thinking that writing for children is easy. However, it's quite the contrary. In order to write for this age group, you must be able to relate to them on their level without talking down to them. You must remember what it was like to be a child and be able to express those feelings in your stories. This large field has its own market guide, *Children's Writer's & Illustrator's Market,* Cincinnati, Ohio, Writer's Digest Books, annual edition.

Interviewing/Profiles

If you enjoy meeting people and exploring their lives, you might want to write profiles. Writing for this field requires that you be able to meet people easily, and acquire an interview with them. Once you've interviewed your subject, taken careful notes, and taped the interview, your job isn't over. It may be necessary for you to interview others who know your subject well. You may also want to become acquainted with the type of work they do by researching the technical aspects of their field. This isn't always necessary. It will depend on how you slant your profile.

Newspaper Columns

To write a regular newspaper column, decide what kind you want to write – humorous, inspirational, informative, current events, church news, etc. Then write the editor a letter explaining what kind of column you'd like to write and how often you could write it. If you have published articles, make copies of them (clips) and include with the letter so the editor can see your writing ability. Explain that you will follow up on your letter by phone (give a certain date, about a week or two) to discuss doing this for the paper. If the editor accepts your offer, you will need to confirm how often your column will run, the deadline for submitting each, the word count length, and what the pay will be for each column. Now, once that's established, write another letter stating the mutual understanding between you and emphasizing that you're ready to begin your career as a newspaper columnist.

Book Reviews

Periodicals that use book reviews will want to see a sample of your writing. If you have published a book review, send a copy of that; if not, send a sample of your best, concise writing. If they like your writing, they will include you on their list of writers to do book reviews for them on assignment. These magazines send you the types of books you have indicated you will review. You keep the books in return for the reviews. Make sure you read the guidelines they provide to know if they accept positive reviews only or critical ones as well. Word count of your review is limited so you must write tight. Deadlines will be critical, some aggressive, and it's important to meet them. When an editor sends you books to review, he will also send a copy of the magazine. Study the book reviews included in the magazine to know the style and content of those published reviews.

Letters to the Editor

Letters to the editor are written in response to something that has appeared in the publication. If an article's content stirs your emotion or passion, you have fuel for this kind of writing. The article may have appeared in a magazine or newspaper. Most publications are happy to receive letters from their readers. Don't write an abusive letter. If your letter overtly offends the editor, it may not get printed. Your letter to the editor is an opportunity to express Christian principles, even if you don't give Scripture references. This can be an avenue for your ministry to that publication's readers. Periodicals, especially daily newspapers, use a great number of letters. Monthly magazines print several letters per issue, making letters to the editor a good area for beginning and experienced writers. You've written letters all your life. Follow their same conversational style when writing letters to the editor.

Travel Writing

If you want to write travel articles, always have paper and a pen or pencil with you on your travels to capture creative ideas as they come to mind. You can turn your traveling experiences into interesting stories.

Make notes of your impressions of the people and places at your destination, noticing unique details. Pick up all available brochures that describe the area and its points of interest and events. These descriptions can help refresh your memory when you return home and sit down to write your article.

Make the readers of your travel article feel like they are where you have been. Use strong verbs and vivid nouns that need little help from adjectives. Include the five senses in your article so the reader will experience as nearly as possible the enjoyment you had on your trip.

Take a camera with you. The pictures you take will also help to refresh your memory as you write. Some magazines pay for photos to use with an article. Be sure to include in your article pertinent operating hours, entrance fees, and toll free telephone numbers for further information about a place or event.

Curriculum Writing

Most large denominations have a church-related publishing house that provides all instructional literature for use in their Sunday schools and other religious education classes. It is imperative that writers of these study guides be familiar with the denomination's beliefs. Independent publishers also produce educational materials and market them across denominational lines.

Church curriculum materials are written for grade or age levels from preschool through senior adults. Publishers print these materials well ahead of their need, working two, five, or ten years in advance. Curriculum writing, therefore, requires assignment writing with exact deadlines.

To get started, request curriculum brochures from those publishers for denominations you are interested in writing for. Curriculum writing is a specialized area. The publisher will supply you with definite content, slant, and guidelines to follow when writing for them.

III

Writing Helps

Market Guides

A current market guide is essential to anyone writing with hopes for publication. A good writers' market guide will include a topical listing of periodicals. Individual magazine listings will include information important to you when deciding where to submit your work for publication. Besides the magazine's address, phone and fax numbers, web site, and email address, you'll find the editorial needs of the magazine, editors' names, denominational affiliation, word count limits, response time, circulation, payment, and whether writers' guidelines and sample copies are available.

Most market guides update their content annually. The publishing business changes rapidly from year to year so be careful not to rely on an outdated edition. Examine the following market guides as you write to publish.

❖ *Christian Writers' Market Guide.* This publication has been compiled for years by Sally E. Stuart. Annual edition. Christian markets only. Listings include book publishers, magazines, gift and specialty markets, electronic contacts, agents, conferences, and writing groups. Beginning in 2012 it will be published by The Christian Writers Guild.

❖ *Writer's Market.* Cincinnati, Ohio: Writer's Digest Books. Annual edition. An exhaustive market guide listing markets in the general field. Also includes agents, national writing awards, and contests. Includes a religious section.

Books for Writers

A vast library of books on the craft of writing is available. For a sample listing log onto Writer's Digest Book Club.

Writers' Magazines

The following magazines provide invaluable information to writers.

❖ *The Christian Communicator.* An informational magazine for the Christian writer and speaker, published eleven times a year by American Christian Writers, Post Office Box 110390, Nashville, TN, 37222, www.ECPA.org/ACW, RegAForder@AOL.com. By subscription.

❖ *The Cross & Quill.* "The Christian writer's newsletter," with articles covering all areas of writing, published bimonthly by the Christian Writer's Fellowship International, 1624 Jefferson

Davis Rd. Clinton, South Carolina 29325-9542,

CWFI@AOL.com,

http://members.aol.com.cwfi/writers.htm. By

subscription.

❖ *Advanced Christian Writer*. A professional
newsletter for the published author, published
bimonthly by American Christian Writers, Post
Office Box 110390, Nashville, TN, 37222,
RegAForder@AOL.com, www.ECPA.org/ACW. By
subscription.

❖ *The Writer*. "Advice and inspiration for today's
writer," published monthly by The Writer, Inc., 120
Boylston Street, Boston, Mass 02116-4615.
Available in bookstores and by subscriptions.
www.writermag.com.

❖ *Writer's Digest*. A "guide to getting published,"
published monthly by F&W Publications, Inc., 1507
Dana Avenue, Cincinnati, Ohio, 45207. Available in

bookstores and by subscription. http://www.writersdigest.com/GeneralMenu/.

❖ *Writers' Journal.* "The complete writer's magazine," published bimonthly by Val-Tech Media, Post Office Box 394, Perham, Minn., 56573-0394. Available in bookstores and by subscription. www.writersjournal.com.

❖ *Online Resource.* Bartleby: Collection of online resources including Strunk & White. http://www.bartleby.com/usage/

Writers' Organizations

It's a good idea to join a local writers' organization if there is one in your area. National organizations also provide benefits helpful to the writer. Here are three:

- ❖ Jerry B. Jenkins Christian Writers Guild, 5525 N. Union Blvd., Ste. 200, Colorado Springs, Colorado 80918.
- ❖ Christian Writer's Fellowship International, 1624 Jefferson Davis Rd., Clinton, South Carolina 29325-9542.
- ❖ American Christian Fiction Writers, P.O. Box 101066, Palm Bay, FL 32910-1066.

Writers' Conferences

Usually held annually, writers' conferences are available around the world. Many writers' magazines and market guides list upcoming conferences. Request brochures from the director of conferences you find interesting. You can also do a search online. A good place to start is Shaw Conferences, http://writing.shawguides.com/.

After you select the writers' conference best suited to your writing goals, paid your registration, and made your hotel reservation and travel plans, you may think you're prepared for the conference. But, before you leave home, let the following tips help you to make the most of attending the conference.

❖ **Plan ahead:** When you receive the conference program, in advance or at the conference, take time to go over the scheduled topics. Tentatively work out your choices, selecting the speakers and subject matter that match your writing interests.

❖ **Go with questions:** Write down questions you need answered. If your questions are not covered in the sessions you attend, ASK. The only dumb question is the one not asked, for it gains no knowledge.

❖ **Take ample supplies:** Take your laptop, if you have one, plenty of paper, pens, and pencils; never rely on just one pen or pencil. You never know what information you might want to jot down, even at breaks and mealtimes; so keep paper handy at all times. If you have business cards take several along. You might meet a writer who has an idea and says he wants to include your writing and asks, "Do you have a card?" When you're talking to an editor, it helps her to remember your name if you can slip her one of your cards. If you don't have business cards, write your name, address, and phone number on some 3x5 cards for this purpose.

❖ **Dress casually:** Registration materials may suggest appropriate dress for the conference. If not, plan to dress casually and wear comfortable shoes. The conference brochure will mention the proper dress for any scheduled banquet or awards dinner.

❖ **Collect guidelines and freebies:** At most writers' conferences, you'll find tables holding free copies of magazines and their writers' guidelines – "freebies." Pick up all the freebies you can carry. Don't browse at the freebie table; you will find more valuable things to do with your time, like meeting with and talking to editors, speakers, published writers, and other attendees. You can sort through your freebies and cull those of interest when you return to your room. You may want to return those freebies you decide not to keep to the freebie table just in case the supplies there run low.

❖ **Take your best writing samples:** Take several copies of your published or unpublished writing samples that editors can look at while you're at the conference or take with them. The writing samples you take should be your best; no first drafts.

❖ **Arrange one-on-one meetings:** Many conferences will make available sign-up sheets where you can select a reserved time to meet with the conference's faculty members. These appointment times are limited so sign up as soon as you arrive at registration time. Take advantage of having a one-on-one with editors and staff. This is an opportunity to have an editor look at your work. You can share an article idea with a magazine editor who may say, "Write it and send it to me."

❖ **Go to learn:** Learning is never finished. Go to the conference to learn your craft of writing. Most conferences hold workshops suitable for beginners as well as for advanced writers. Read the conference brochure carefully before registration to make sure of the conference's focus.

❖ **Participate:** Don't allow yourself any idle time; participate fully. You can rest when you get home. Even if none of the workshops offered in a time slot interest you, pick one to attend anyway. You might decide you could branch out into different areas with your writing.

❖ **Talk to the faculty:** Talk to the staff, faculty, and speakers on the program. They're interested in writers or they wouldn't be there. Talk to them at lunch, breaks, autograph times, and after they speak. Making these contacts is called "networking," a valuable tool for becoming a published writer. Above all, don't be shy; be bold, aggressive! Take advantage of all their knowledge just waiting to be tapped by you.

❖ **Meet other attendees:** Introduce yourself to other conference attendees. If you make an acquaintance, the two of you can share notes by attending different sessions scheduled for the same time. Exchange addresses (don't forget email addresses). This gives you writer friends to correspond with; it's like having a long-distance writing group.

❖ **Write thank-you letters:** Follow up with thank-you notes or letters to faculty who have shared their time and knowledge with you, whether in a general session or at a one-on-one appointment. And don't forget to thank the hardworking director and her staff.

Writers' conferences are invaluable to the beginning and the seasoned writer both in knowledge gained and contacts made. Many publications no longer accept unsolicited manuscripts. Meeting an editor face to face at a conference will help you get over that hurdle when submitting your work.

Plan ahead and avail yourself of all that a writers' conference offers. You can return home with new ideas, increased knowledge, and greater confidence in your writing ability.

But you must follow through with the resolves you've been inspired to make while at the conference. When you get home, don't delay. Write!

IV

Glossary

A - Z

All rights: The total sale of your written work; you give up all control of it.

Byline: The author's name placed immediately below the title of your work.

Circulation: Copies distributed of one issue of a publication.

Contributor's copy: A copy of the issue of a periodical in which the author's work appears.

Copyright: Legal protection of ownership by the author of a work.

Cover letter: A letter that the author includes when submitting a manuscript.

Devotional: A short piece that reflects on a writer's personal experience and insight into that experience.

Electronic submission: Submitting a work to an editor or publisher by email or on a disk.

First rights: Gives an editor the exclusive right to publish your work for the first time.

Freelance writer: A writer who markets his work to publishers but is not on salary.

On acceptance: Payment is made when work is accepted for publication.

On assignment: Writing a work upon the request of an editor.

One-time rights: The right for editors to publish a work one time, knowing it has already sold first rights.

On publication: Payment is made when work is published.

Reprint rights: Selling the right to reprint a work that has already been published after waiting until it has been published the first time.

SAE: Self-addressed envelope (without stamps).

SASE: Self-addressed, stamped envelope.

Simultaneous submission: Sending the same work to more than one publisher at the same time. In your cover letter inform the editor you're making a simultaneous submission.

Take-home paper: A periodical available to Sunday school children and adults to take home.

Writers' guidelines: A listing of a publication's instructions for writing for that publication.